Soul Whispers

by

Nancy Alhabashi

Soul Whispers
By Nancy Alhabashi

First Printing
Copyright 2011 ©
ISBN 978-1-937118-02-0
Printed in USA by
Creative Book Printing
   of Budget Transfer Printing & Bindery
Stone Mountain, GA 30087
www.budgettransfer.com
02-2012

For more information and additional copies,
contact Nancy Alhabashi, marwa221@hotmail.com
http://artbreak.com/marwa or www.NancyAlhabashi.com

Dedication

To my father, who lives in my heart.
To you Mother, I love you.

Soul Whispers

Your Love is a Miracle
Once upon a time there was a tree on a moon
Once upon a time a tree fell down from the moon
Once upon a time you loved me

Tell Me

Tell me, Oh dear, tell me
Do I love you? Ask a bird
If he loves to fly
Ask the moon
How come it stays up high
Tell me, Oh dear tell me
Do I love you
Ask an angel and devil too
How come people look the way they do
Oh dear, Tell me no more
For your love with me
All mysteries will devour

Let's Pretend

Time has always wondered
When our love will end
I laughed
One of life wonders is love
One of earth tragedies is unborn love
Let's pretend that we both never met
And meet all over again...

Found

When a man finds his love
Wind asks "trees! Will you dance with me?"

Mommy

Mommy, mommy
What have you done?
Tell me; is it true
That you are gone?
You had me once
and said goodbye
You turned your back
I don't know why
Where is my milk
God Gave you much
I want to drink
There is no more!
O, mommy, mom
I am only four
Not years not days
I am four of months
Don't shut the door
My life is worth
Sixteen you are
But you're my mom
Come back, come back
Don't do me harm
I love my grandma
But it's not the same

She feeds me milk
Not mommy's love
No mistake, I'm a gift
From God above
Take care of me
Don't say goodbye
I'm so much joy
I am so much fun
I'll make you smile
I'll walk and run
I'll make you proud
Of me one day
When I can write
When I can say
A word you wrote
I am too much work
Right now I know
But don't forget
That easy come
Will easy go
Just look at me
And see your eyes
I've got your smile
In different size
I love you please
Don't say goodbye

A Tree and Two Roads

Two roads to take stop to decide.
A tree in a distance, big, green and wide.

A rest you need before you plan.
A destiny for a woman and a man.

Let shades of tree cool off your face.
Where lines of sweat made a keenly trace.

When following destiny, when wanting light.
All heart beats abide all evils fight.

It takes two hands when promise done.
It takes two hearts to join as one.

Keep up the trust, faith and love.
Keep up the hope, pray to above.

The songs we sang, the words we felt.
Were a thousand bricks to the home we built.

To promise love and give your heart.
Ain't a laughing matter, or an acting part.

These vows are watched by God in heaven.
These vows are blessed with number seven.

A journey if felt its depth so true.
Angels will accompany, God will too.

Rest and shade under that tree.
Once road is chosen, heart is free.

Let's start first step on that long road.
and a gold lace sheet wraps a love untold.

Little White Room

In a little white room, they broke the news
And said I have cancer
In a little white room, I got confused
My heart beat faster
In a little white room, I held my tears
From falling harder
I looked around in a silent room
For a way to get me fast at home
They told me not to leave right now
There's many more tests to show us how
You've got your mass with needles. Aw!
Don't keep me here, I cannot bare
To stay so far from kids I bare
I need them now to spend sometime
My clock is clicking, ah that's not fair
I need their smile to help me through
I need their words, their faces too
How could I be a falling tree
for a blooming branch trying to see
The world of life, oh God help me

A Song of Hope

I will come back, don't say goodbye
Few months of chemo and time will fly
Take care of Daddy, your sisters too
Be good my son, don't fuss don't cry
Some things must happen don't ask me why
I taught your nanny your songs at night
I've shown her how to hold you tight
I urge you please to stay so strong
And sing with me a wishful song
A song of hope, to bring me back
To help you grow through life alone
I love you son, in good and bad
So help me through it, don't get so sad
No tears I am asking, no sighs at all
Let's pray together, please hold my hand
Don't cry my son, if I come not
I'll watch you there, I'll miss you but
It will be hard, yet you should know
That's life sometimes is a painful show
It's hard and tough, but there is more
Than that in life, of that I'm sure
I love you son, you are my cure.

What If

What if the apple did not fall
And Newton didn't wonder
What if Einstein erased it all
And Apollo didn't show Alexander
We've learned so much along the way
Let go of things that should've stayed
What if, I wonder
We've dug so deep, and reached the moon
We've known when rain will come so soon
We knew it all why did we keep
The good and bad, yet we will weep
For a tree that shed our home before
The letters we've written to friends and more
If knowledge come not at all
How far, dear, think you'll be now
Like a sword it cuts back and forth
We need it much, but is it worth
The souls we lost, in world of war
Or a time we missed with son to adore
TV and net and mobile too
That's why we let our neighbors go
Oh knowledge, dear, what have you done
Oh knowledge, dear
Oh knowledge dear

It's Over

No more poetry
No more tears
No more worries
Not even fears
Our love is over
Our love is dead
So good together
That's what we were
My soul was lost
Not here or there
Love is so sweet
In one condition
If being your self
Doesn't need permission

Eternal
If I ever decide to leave you
I will take you with me...

Dreams

Dreams are more real than awakening
For dreams, feelings are not censored
And fear of judgment does not exist
When a man dreams
His real feelings abide
And he acts upon it

Better World

Good deeds are like feathers in a pillow
We have to have so many
To make a difference
A man of good deeds
Is like a lonely flower on a desert rock

Your Cup of Coffee
Your cup of coffee
Is calling me "Good Morning"
Your boiling eggs are waiting for
A breakfast we had
Your pots, your chair
Are screaming mad
"Where did she go?"
Your skin is crying sad
For a touch of mine
Your kiss is haunting you
For my neck for my hand
Your prayers are hoping
Are asking God
To bring me back
Against the odds

Floating

I am a floating rose in your garden
I am a bird
I am cloud
I am a mountain
I am a river
I am a fountain
I am everything
For you in here
One, two, three.
Please, stop counting
I am everything
I am anything
In your world

Silent Symphony

Wisdom once said, if talk is silver, silence is gold
Like gold and silver, we're bought and sold
We're thrown at rocks, we're thrown on feathers
To the left to the right, stand still? Will never
With broken hearts we stand alone
With falling tears our love has gone
Through life alone, we cry forever
We smile sometimes, we laugh together
We yell, we sing, we stumble and utter
Some people sing for us to sooth
Our open cuts, does it work? oh never
If a voice come not from down within
A singing rhyme like a streaming river
It feels you not, it heels you not
Once self is heard you're blessed forever
It's silent symphony from God above
To help us stand when life is bitter

I Love You

I love you through my dreams
I love you through my night
Your whispers kiss my ears
So crazy we become
No rules no wrongs no rights

Waiting

A flower stands above a pond
It is passed by so many
It is stared at by so many
Beneath the water its root calmly lays
Beneath the water its soul wears a hoping dress,
Restful face
Praying for that one true believer
Waiting for that strong admirer
Searching for that one beauty seeker
Graciously its waiting
Waiting….
Waiting….

Your Presence

Your presence is as warm
as a cozy room in a chilly night
what is home?
it's your smell, your voice, your sight
love me, please
left to right
dress me colors,
black, and white
for love, there is not
wrong or right

Freedom

I was in Cairo in mid January
Then one month later I was in Tripoli
I walked with those who walked the line
Go out dear kingdoms, the streets are mine
I'm full of passion when they are asleep
In the midst of sadness I will not weep
My name is freedom I live in Jail
My path is always in rocky trail
I stood by Martin when he once said
I have a dream that I shall defend
You find me with those who once dare
To form the line in Tahrir square
My name is freedom I'm not for free
It takes many lives for me to be
Pack up your crowns Its time to pay
You will be leaving I am here to stay

Hidden

Your love is hidden beneath
your love is a secret
a question to release
you can't dare ask it
your love is hidden
your love is forbidden
your love is a secret.

A Woman
Touch me like a flower
Smell me like one
Breathe me through the rain shower
When the winter begins
Hold me close
Kiss me on
My lips my cheeks
My neck my chin
Ah how could I deny
Ah how could I run
From a love that made
Me a puzzle to undone
A shining moon
A star, a sun
A whole with you
A unit of you
A woman

Back in the Years
       so much has happened
But we tend to forget
We tend to lie to our souls
That our bodies have no cuts
Maybe true to flesh and blood
But for hearts, Oh not at all
Words were said to hurt before
It may hide there beneath our skin
But deep inside it'll grow and crawl

A poem is like a woman,
>> she puts on her wedding dress when it
>> Is written, and takes it off when it is read....

*W*ords are always better written than said.

*O*nce upon a time there were me and you
Then we became one
Then two again

I have heard my door sing as you entered my room
I have felt my cup of coffee trembling when it touched your
lips
My walls cried and my curtains fell when you said goodbye.
Come back again not because I missed you, because I missed
my old happy home too.

DON'T

Don't speak
Just look
I read your eyes
Like an open book
    Don't ask
    Command
    I'll walk your path
    When you hold my hand
        Don't rush
        Love me slow
        For seconds are hours
        When you go
            Don't say goodbye
            And welcome me
            Let's fly like birds
            So high and free
        Don't try
            Just do
            and love me
            as much
            as I love you

Valentine

When you pour love into my cup,
 I can't dare drink
When you speak to me
I would not think
When I look at you
I would not blink

Tulip

The tens of tulips gathered under the sun
A solid army of color that speaks to the soul
To celebrate our every day
Be safe for me I love you
I love you

Son's of Earth

I cried "my children have begun to slip away"
"That's life" you said, "it's quite okay"
I can't deny your words are true
Yet, it hurts to let them go
Don't hold on tight to kids you've raised
Just raise them well, and say goodbye
They'll come back then and thank you for
How much you've given, and not incur
It's easy said, and may be cruel
That they belong
To the life of all
Not mine not yours
They're sons of earth
To feel and grow in God's rules
Their spirits will shine
Future will see, but we will not
"Don't cry my dear"
You said to me
"You've done the same"
Back in the years
Our sons we fed them love and joy
One day they will give it back
To sons of earth
Which whom they've raised.

My father

I miss you father
Where did you go?
I miss you much
Where did you go?
An oak tree told me
You went away
To the other side
That does not say
That does not tell
That does not show
I miss you father
Where did you go?

I missed your frown
That told me much
I missed your smile
I missed you much

I asked the sky
Have you seen my father?
She gently shook
And threw a ladder
She hollered come
And see your dad
I dare not go
Forgive me dad

When my time comes
I'll see you then
So rest in peace
Till after then

For the memory of the most loving father on earth

Ordinary
How many
heroes
through
the circle
of time
were left
unknown?

Smile

Smile
So the birds can fly
And sing above the Nile
Smile, please
Would you......

Blessed

White is your veil
Pure is your heart
I sinned
Blessed let me be
A journey to begin
Clean path, holy start

I have touched eternity,
>   when I wiped off my child's falling tear.
I have seen glory,
>   when I saw a woman give birth to a child.
I have felt love,
>   when you heard my heart beating by looking at me.

Loving is giving
Giving is when you don't expect something back

A woman's heart is like the ocean.
If a ship sinks it will never leave.
A man's heart is like a harbor
a ship sails today, another arrives tomorrow

Daddy

There are no more words of you to utter
Or laughs, and smiles and time together
Don't worry my dad I'm doing fine
I 'm getting stronger through life of mine
Your time was up, did not thank you for
A life you gave me, and love to adore
I love you daddy, God took you fast
But gave me a son who looks like you at last
You're gone away, but you're in him
Your smile your eyes, I see you in them
He's got your voice your silence too
Oh thank you God for a gift so true
For a beautiful soul it could be what
I've lost of you father don't forget
You'll stay with me, so long right here
As a son of mine, I love you dear

When I am with You
I am a bumble bee
Jumping from rose to rose
in your soul
When I am with you
I'm a bunch of words
to the book of all
I am everything, I'm a child, I'm a doll
I am a beautiful mole that's always there
I shall breathe not if you don't share
With me your wall
The wall of love
Which I will crawl
If you must go
My tear will fall
My life will be
An empty hole

A man should give his heart only
not to the woman who could make him cry.
But to the woman who can Hear him cry.

A silent word sometimes is
louder than thousands of screams.
Only if it is said with a glance to the beloved.

Garden of Love

The garden of love blossoms in the presence of the beloved
Trees bow to feel earth welcoming its presence
Lilies and roses hug like lovers in a summer night...
in the beloved presence....love abides

Like You Never Loved Before
In the glory of love
I have found you
I have wanted you
I have needed you
A man is complete
For his love is there
A man is holy
For feelings to despair
For a smile to desire
For a touch, for a spirit higher
Than me and you
Than Universe
Than a child, than a mother
Than death than life
Than all combined
I love you
Love me back
Like you never loved before

Laugh

Laugh please

Laugh please

My world becomes a garden

Of butterflies when you do so

Surrender

When your love takes over
I hold up my white flag.

You'll Never Die

Shall I swear off a glance that shook me?
Or a smile that stayed with me
Shall I love you as you are?
Shall I be you?
For you my love
You are forbidden
For you my love
You are never here
For you my love
I can never smell
I can never touch
I can never feel

> Have you left too early?
> Have you gone with no alarm?
> For your body is a mist
> And you memory is eternal

Be born again in a bird's song
Or even in a rose smell
Be born like an angel
Who never dies......

Celebration

Nights were made for
The stars to celebrate the presence of the moon.

Lust
I will burn one day
Because I love you

Lost

When a man loses his love, earth weeps,
Autumn saddens,
And refuses to throw his leaves
Winter cries,
Spring dies,
And summer leaves

Space

I lost you once up in space
No vision of you nor trace
I've shown you love
You have not seen
I've spoken words
You thought I lied
Why did you? Why did I
Lose you once up in the sky?

Why

With a trembling thought
And a heart that fought
I loved you
With a cause untold
And silent word
You left me
You said goodbye
To the words we said
To the laughs
To the songs
To a love we've raised
To the books we've read
You went so far
How could you
You came back soon
Why did you
How come you've missed
Those lips you've kissed
Don't lie
But now it's me who says goodbye
And now it's me who wonders why
I loved you.

Crazy
My friend is crazy
And
I
am
the
crazy
lover

Away

you're gone away
but you're still here
your things are there
your steps are there
your breath is there
but you're still here
you're still as charming
when you lead my thoughts
you're still as calming
with words you wrote
you've gone away
but you're still here
with her you left
and said goodbye
should have said hello
for you live in my heart
no matter where you go

Little White Lie
When it's time to leave
Don't tell me
Let me think that you're still around

Foolish Word

For a foolish word I have said once
You left
Where are you?
Sitting or standing
Passing or staying
Where are the kisses
Where are the flowers
Take all my sorrys
Take all my pleases
Why?
It was just a foolish word I have said......

Poison

Push me, oh love, push me
Away
Your love is poisonous
Your love is mad
Are you killing enough of me
Push me, oh love, away
For I will not leave
Unless you push me away

Let's be friends
My red roses, they all turned pale
Dresses in my closet, they all look ugly
My favorite chocolate, suddenly tastes plain
All of my dreams have sad endings
   My nights seem longer
   My days are lightless
   I hate my books
   Dislike my looks
   My rooms curtains
   Is all I see
   The sorrow whispers
   Is all I hear
My big failure is all I feel
One little sentence
Turned off my heart
Now my life ends
Yes, when you said
   "Let's be just friends"

Unhappy

Although I am wearing my happy dress,
Yet, I am not happy
My laughter holds tears beneath, and
My happy songs are crying.
My hope is trying
My bird isn't flying
Although I am wearing my happy dress,
Yet, I am not happy

Ancient
I see my father's frown
in the smile of my unborn son.
I see some happy tears
I see weeping cheers
I see you
I see my father in my unborn son
I feel you I hear you
Like a rising sun
I see you Ancient
I see you loud and silent
I see you clear
I see you close
I see you far
I see you Ancient
Since the start of time
I see you father

He Loves You More

My father died
   And left us all
   To cry behind him
   And grieve his soul
My father died
   But he did not
   His soul is here
   We love you but
God loves you more

Sister

Where are you sister
To remember with me my early years
Where are you sister
To hear my laughter
And touch my falling tears
Where is our childhood
Has it been that long
Where is our laughter
And crying song
Where are you sister
To keep me strong
I miss our childhood
I miss you too
Let's dance forever
So fast, so slow
And sing together
Like children do!

Earth

Tell me Earth, What have you seen through the time
She said: I have seen much
        I have seen so little
I said:
What is there to be told and remembered?
She said:

        A hand that reached for the needy
        And a word that was spoken for the lonely
        And a smile that was given to a child.

Storm

life is like a storm
you never know when it will hit
when it will rise when it will sit
one day we're floating
one day we're drowning
trying to live it
like runnels of water
streaming
doesn't stop
doesn't end
doesn't quit

Burning

Truth will hurt like a burning fire
yet, I would love to know
tell me once
        or tell me twice
for fire is cooler than a calming ice
truth will hurt
        but it will show
who loves you not
        or loves you so
burn me please
        and let me know
touch my ears
        and touch my soul
               and let me know
                  of it all

In the Past
Future will be present,
Present will go now,
Past will stay forever!
You and I will laugh together
Yet, we may never see each other
Like forever;
So close, so distant
So sweet, so bitter.

Squares

prisoners we are
in dragging thoughts of race
yet, we deny
different but we all have face
with eyes
you'll hide but
your smile will show
it's fake it's cold
we feel it though
no matter what
I'll forgive you for
human we are
no less, no more

Peace
Once the sky asked Earth
"What is the holy land waiting for?"
-"for peace, love and harmony."
-How long will she be waiting?"
Earth smiled and did not answer.

We are All One
Angels of peace appear
When the line of the different disappear
Why can't all belong to humanity
Why can't we all dissolve

Modesty

Kings become royal, when majesty of the kings
Appears in a poor man presence

A Letter from an Ordinary Mother
My children are all gone
In the midst of time, to return
Back to me men and women of life.

Peace of Mind
A poor man envies the rich
      The rich man envies pillows with sleeping eyes

Your Words are Wonder

Your smile is under
My pillow it sleeps
Your glance, it keeps
My heart beating like thunder

A Letter from a Dead Man
I long to peaceful nights
I long to wrongs and rights
I long to you
I long to yellow
I long to blue

> I long to life
> I long to family,
> To son and wife

I long to truth
I long to lies
I long to misery
In a lost child's eyes

> I long to everything
> When nothing is all I have

Steal
me
from
under
my
blanket
and
make
me
a
jailed
pigeon
in
your
house.

Forbidden Love

Oh love but not me, for I am forbidden
Oh, kiss not my lips for you to reach heaven
A sin we are, a secret, a lie within
If love were to write, our names are written
If love were to be, beneath its hidden
For love so strong, yet so hopeless
No bridge of earth will reach unless
We hurt him and her, and evil will bless
Stand dear away
For our love may
Only live forbidden

Little Lie

I love you darling where did you go
Why did you leave me, you killed me slow
Why did you hurt the child in me
Why did your eyes another see
How did she make you forget the times
We shared together, our songs our rhymes
how dare you give our dreams to her
how dare you kiss her lips how dare
don't say goodbye just leave me silent
I'll tell my books my walls my walnut
He's leaving for sometimes because
He wants to bring a beautiful rose
From far away, at another world
He wants to learn some songs to sing
In my day of birth so much he'll bring

Mortal

Mankind a is a mix of emotions
Mortal who can hide both
Mortal who can cry with no tears
Mortal who can cover all his fears
Mortal who dies so silent
And not be heard
And rise so softly
Like a flying bird

Real beauty comes only from within, it resides in every human heart. You can't touch it. You can't see it. You can only feel it.

When a man relies on others to make choices for him,
he becomes the product of their thoughts.

When you build a home based on love, you build a castle.

Because we can only forgive and not forget;
forgiveness means giving away anger when remembering.

He who does not see the color of others,
love will reside in his heart forever.

Strength has 2 brothers and 2 sisters:
Hope and Knowledge. Hard Work and Coexistence.

Melody
My dreams were silent
till you appeared
sounds of violin
at night is heard
beams in my heart
plays at night
every glorious tune
every singing groan
every string I played
every love parade
no one so much as you
my life has changed

When You Cry

Clouds will rain
When you speak
Shores will strain
When you sleep
The moon will wane
When you smile
Birds will sing
Please smile again
When you pray
The world repeats "Amen"

About the Author

Nancy Alhabashi, poet, painter, artist and designer,
originally from Nazareth,
resides in Lawrenceville, Georgia
with her husband
and three little ones.